A
Gentleman's
Code

A
GENTLEMAN'S
CODE

according to Confucius, Mencius and Others

ed. Philip Chew Kheng Hoe

Graham Brash (Pte) Ltd
Singapore

© *Selection and arrangement of quotations,*
Philip Chew Kheng Hoe, 1984

Published by Graham Brash (Pte) Ltd
36-C Prinsep St
Singapore 0718

ISBN 9971 947 67 6

Typeset and printed by Lolitho Pte Ltd

Contents

Confucius　　　　　　　　　　*1*

Mencius　　　　　　　　　　*35*

Others　　　　　　　　　　*48*

Preface

A book of quotations is a treasure house of wit and wisdom, not to be plundered all at once, but to be visited again and again, each individual gem to be taken up, examined and admired. It is also good advice not only to remember the quotations for their intrinsic value but also to try and put them into practice.

This selection deals with only one topic — the Gentleman. (It need hardly be said that all his aims and ideals apply equally to the Lady or Gentlewoman.) It is a topic which I believe can never be exhausted.

I have tried to make this selection as comprehensive as possible and I present it so that the writers, poets and philosophers of yesterday and today may speak to you. If reading this book gives you as much pleasure as preparing it has given me, I shall be more than rewarded.

Philip Chew Kheng Hoe

.... according to Confucius

He who can appreciate men of virtue as he can appreciate women of beauty, who in serving his parents exerts himself to the utmost, who in serving his country is ready to sacrifice his life, who in his dealings with his friends is found trustworthy — such a one, though unschooled, may be considered a gentleman.

Is it not indeed a pleasure to study with constant perseverance and having acquired knowledge, to put it into practice?

A great man feels no discomposure when others fail to appreciate his ability and integrity.

A young man's duty is to be filial to his parents and respectful to his elders, to be circumspect at all times, to feel for and assist his fellowmen. Let him devote whatever time and energy he has to spare to literary and artistic pursuits.

A gentleman daily examines his personal conduct on three points: In carrying out the duties entrusted to him by others, has he failed in conscientiousness? In dealing with his friends, has he failed in sincerity and faithfulness? In all his dealings, has he failed to pass on whatever he has learned which may assist others?

Observe what a man has in mind to do when his father is living and then observe his conduct when his father is dead. If, for three years after his father's death, he does not deviate from the principle of his father's ways, he is entitled to be called a good son.

If a man makes promises within the bounds of what is right, he will be able to keep his word. If he demonstrates respectfulness and propriety according to the Rites (rules of social conduct, Ceremonies or Rituals), he need never feel shame or disgrace. If he cultivates ties with those with whom intimacy is proper, he will never be dishonoured.

A person who lacks gravity does not inspire respect.

Make loyalty and sincerity your guiding principles in life. Have no friends who are not as good as you. When you have erred, do not hesitate to rectify your mistake. Aim not only for success but to be of value to your fellowmen.

The manner in which a gentleman seeks information is different from the manner in which other men seek it. He obtains it by being gracious, simple, earnest and courteous.

One who is not greedy or slothful but active and earnest, who is cautious in his speech and seeks out the company of men of virtue and learning — such a one is truly eager to learn.

A gentleman is not concerned about others not knowing him. His great concern is his not knowing how to be an ideal gentleman.

A virtuous man is like the North Polar Star which keeps its position while all the other stars are attracted towards it.

If a ruler depends entirely on laws and punishments, the common people will stay out of trouble but they will have no sense of shame for wrongdoing. If, on the other hand, a ruler depends on virtue and encourages observation of the Rites,

*wrongdoers will not only feel ashamed but will
reform themselves.*

*At fifteen one should devote oneself to serious
studies. At thirty one's character is formed. At forty
life has fewer perplexities. At fifty one should
understand the will and decrees of Heaven. At sixty
one's ears should be attuned to them. At seventy,
one's thoughts should be able to wander without
moral transgression.*

*Filial piety requires that children should serve their
parents when they are alive in accordance with the
Rites, bury them when they die in accordance with
the Rites, and thereafter honour their memories in
accordance with the Rites.*

*A man should take such care of himself that his
parents need have no anxiety concerning him.*

*Look closely at how a person behaves; mark his
motives; observe his pleasures. How thus can his
true character evade you?*

*Be versed in ancient ideas and familiarise yourself
with the new. Then may you become a worthy
teacher of men.*

If a son merely ensures that his parents have enough to eat and there is no deep feeling of love and respect towards them, wherein lies the difference between his relationship with them and his relationship with his domestic animals?

No man is a machine. He should not behave heartlessly like one, or as if others were machines.

Study and intelligence are inter-dependent. Studying without thinking brings bewilderment. Thinking without learning from others (this is the essence of studies) can be dangerous.

A great man can see a question from all sides without bias. A mean man cannot.

It can be harmful to come, without thought, under the sway of utterly new and strange doctrines.

This is wisdom: when you are aware of what you know, to maintain that you know it; and when you do not, to acknowledge your ignorance.

Read and learn everything you can, but suspend judgement if you are in doubt. Be cautious in what

*you say. In that way your mistakes will be few.
Widen your experience, but beware of hazardous
places and always give heed to where you wander.
In that way you will seldom have occasion for
regret.*

*Let experience guide our words and actions, and let
our actions reinforce our words.*

*By being a good citizen and practising brotherhood,
one can exert an influence upon government. In so
doing, one is, in fact, taking part in government.*

*I do not see how a person can be acceptable if his
words cannot be trusted. A cart without a yoke and
a horse without a harness — how can the cart be
expected to move?*

*It is moral cowardice to be faced with what is right
and leave it undone.*

*If a man is without a sense of what
is right and wrong, what can he do
with the Rites? How can he have
any sense of propriety?*

In the practice of the Rites it is better to be simple than extravagant; in those which relate to mourning it is better that there should be genuine sorrow than minute attention to traditional observances.

A gentleman does not compete merely for the sake of competition. He competes for the sake of the sport and is therefore a true sportsman.

If one cannot pray with heart and soul, it is as if one has not prayed at all.

The emotion of love in a gentleman is passionate but not sensual, and sad also, without being painful.

There is nowhere to turn to in prayer if one has offended against God.

How should one regard a man who, in possession of power, lacks benevolence; who, in ceremonial performance, lacks reverence; and who, in mourning, lacks heartfelt grief?

Virtue is never alone. A good man is bound to attract other good men.

A virtuous man is one who loves a moral life and hates an immoral life. One who finds virtue attractive would never let any other considerations come first. One who hates an immoral life would not allow evil to contaminate him. Well, is there any man who is able for one whole day to exert himself thus?

A gentleman finds peace of mind in virtue and he covets it.

If a wealthy man sets his mind on benevolence, he will be free from evil.

If a man forsakes Virtue, how is he to fulfil the obligations of his name! Even in moments of haste and hurry, even in moments of danger and peril, let him keep true to Virtue.

Few are competent to love and to hate others.

A man's faults are peculiar to his class and environment. By observing a man's faults one can come to understand his good points.

He has not lived in vain who dies the day he has learnt the Truth.

*One who is intent upon learning the moral life and
yet is ashamed of wearing shabby clothes and
eating coarse food is not worthy of being called
a scholar in search of truth.*

*Likes and dislikes should not affect our judgement.
We should be on the side of what is right and
against what is wrong.*

*A virtuous man cherishes his soul, the mean man
cherishes earthly things. A virtuous man respects
the law, the mean man thinks of how he may
circumvent it for his personal gain.*

*A gentleman understands what is moral; a base
man understands what is advantageous or
profitable.*

*When one meets with men of worth, one should try
to emulate them. When one meets worthless men,
one should look within and examine oneself for
similar weaknesses and vices.*

*In serving his parents, a man may on occasion
offer gentle remonstrances, but if he sees that his
advice is being ignored, he should nevertheless still*

continue to show them reverent respect, never discourtesy. However much anxiety or suffering they cause, let him care for them without complaining or murmuring.

While his parents are alive, a man should not venture too far in his travels. If he does, he should let them know where he is sojourning.

One should always bear in mind the age of one's parents. On the one hand, their age is an occasion for rejoicing that they have seen so many years. On the other hand, it is a cause for anxiety that so few years remain.

A wise man does not readily give utterance to words in case his actions do not live up to his words.

A gentleman is slow to speak but prompt to act.

To be daring is not enough. One must exercise judgement in the course of being daring.

Wealth and honour acquired by unrighteous means are like drifting clouds.

*In our early dealings with men, our attitude is to
listen to their words and trust their conduct. With
experience, our attitude now is to listen to their
words and observe their conduct.*

*A gentleman's code of conduct is not to do unto
others what he does not want others to do unto
him.*

*The four essential virtues of a leader are that in his
personal conduct he is respectful; in his dealings
with his inferiors he is considerate; in caring for
the welfare of the common people he is generously
kind; and in dealing with all, he is just.*

*However long a man has known his friends, he
should always treat them with the same scrupulous
courtesy. In this way familiarity will not breed
contempt but greater admiration.*

*A gentleman's way of acquiring knowledge and
wisdom is to be industrious, fond of learning,
and unashamed to ask questions of those who are
superior to him.*

*Let your scholarship be that of a great gentleman,
not that of a mere gentleman.*

He who wishes to live a good life must first be conscious of any faults within himself. Only after struggling to overcome these faults will he attain goodness.

What a gentleman most desires is to be a comfort to his aged parents at home, a trusworthy friend to those without, and a source of affection and kindness to all.

During calamity, a good leader does everything possible to help the really needy; he does not strive to make the rich more rich.

It is indeed a well-balanced admixture of nature and nurture that will result in the perfect gentleman.

Those who know a subject are not like those who love it; those who love it are not like those who find their joy in it day and night. Thus it is possible for a teacher to discourse on higher subjects with those who are above average, but not with those who are below average.

To labour for the promotion of righteous conduct

and to hold in awe and reverence the gods and spirits of the universe are the duties of a gentleman.

If a leader has unworthy motives, may God reject him, may God reject him!

I murmur not against God, nor complain against men. In my studies, learning from the lowest and the highest, I have come to acquire knowledge of what is noble and lofty. Only in this manner can God help me.

One can always learn something from others. One can profit by good examples and avoid bad examples.

In this world one cannot hope to meet God; the most one can hope for is to meet a sage.

Those who are busy and active enjoy life; those who are calm and quiet are long-lived.

There are some who act without understanding, but a gentleman is not like that. He reads and learns everything and, selecting what is excellent, he follows it. He sees everything and takes note of what he sees.

Prayer is not confined to the moments spent in a temple but expresses itself in every thought, word and action.

A gentleman is composed and happy; a mean man is always full of anxiety.

Unless a man has the spirit of the Rites, in being courteous he will wear himself out, in being cautious he will become timid, in being bold he will become reckless, and his frankness will become effrontery.

When a bird is about to die, its song is sad; when a man is about to die, his words are worth listening to.

A gentleman tries to banish from his bearing all traces of violence and arrogance, to remove from his actions all insincerity, to purge from his speech all vulgarity and impropriety.

A leader must be strong and bold, for his burden is heavy and he has far to go. His duty to his

*fellowmen is the burden, and is that not heavy?
Only with death does his journey end. Is the way
then not a long and weary one?*

*If one has admirable gifts and yet is arrogant or
mean, then all the rest of one's qualities are not
worth speaking of.*

*I cannot understand those who are enthusiastic and
yet not straightforward, nor those who are ignorant
and yet not cautious, nor again those who are
simple-minded and yet without honesty.*

*In the course of your education, study as though
time is short and as though apprehensive of not
reaching your goal in time.*

*There are four things a man of superior mind
eschews: he takes nothing for granted, he is never
over-positive, he is never inflexible and he is never
egotistic.*

*If a gentleman were to go and dwell among
uncivilised tribes, how could they be crude? His
very character would reform them.*

Is knowledge of the truth instinctive? No. Only by

*considering both the pros and cons of a question
can one get to the bottom of the matter.*

*There are, are there not, young plants that fail
to produce blossoms, and blossoms that fail to
produce fruit? Similarly with respect to the careers
of my students and disciples.*

*Youth should be regarded with some awe. How
does one know what the future holds in store? Only
when a man reaches forty or fifty without having
done anything to distinguish himself does he cease
to deserve to be held in awe.*

*A gentleman desires most to excel in moral rather
than sexual prowess.*

*There are those who study but are not yet able to
grasp the Truth; there are those who can grasp the
Truth but are not yet able to take a firm stand
regarding it; there are those who can take such a
firm stand but are not yet able to exercise
judgement.*

*The wise are free from perplexity, the good from
anxiety and the brave from fear.*

Until we have learned to serve the living, how can we hope to serve the spirits of the dead properly? We do not as yet understand even life; how can we hope to comprehend death?

It is the mark of a gentleman that he is chary of speech. When to act is difficult, is it any wonder that he is chary of talking about it?

A man who conducts himself with earnestness and courtesy will find all men within the Four Seas (the world) his brothers. What reason then has he to worry just because he has no brothers in his home?

The real quality of a man is the stuff he is made of during a severe crisis.

Let the ruler be as a ruler; let the minister be as a minister; let the father be as a father; let the son be as a son; let the gentleman be as a gentleman. If not, would there be concord in the land?

When a man examines himself and discovers no guilt in his heart, why should he be anxious or afraid?

In the conduct of government as of one's personal life, ponder untiringly over the plans and then conscientiously carry them out.

There are three essentials to good government: sufficient food for all, a strong army and the good faith of the people. Without the trust of the people, there can be no government.

A gentleman helps others to realise what is good in them; he does not help others to discover their weaknesses and failings.

A good leader may be compared to the wind and the common people to the grass. Let the wind blow over the grass and the grass, under the force of the wind, cannot but bend.

A true leader of men does not seek popularity, but righteousness. His goal is not a high position, but the opportunity to perform meritorious deeds.

What should one do to improve one's character, correct one's

personal faults and dispel the delusions of life?
First, make it a rule not to accept
any reward unless you have worked hard to earn
it. That is the best way to honour and virtue.
Secondly, vanquish your own vices and failings
before condemning those of others. That is the best
way to remove the secret vices of the innermost
mind. And thirdly, do not let sudden anger
endanger your safety or that of your loved ones.

In his conduct with his friends, a gentleman should
be frank in what he says. He should try to guide
them discreetly towards what is good, but he
should stop if there is no hope of success, and not
court humiliation.

In the society of books, a cultivated man wins
friends; in the society of friends, he is furthering
goodwill among people of all nationalities.

One should begin by defining all things accurately.
If a thing is not correctly defined, what is said will
not correspond with the facts. When words do not
correspond with facts, affairs will not culminate in
success. When affairs do not succeed, order and
harmony cannot flourish, law and justice will not

fit the crime. When law and justice do not fit the crime, mankind is in confusion.

If a leader's personal conduct is upright, the common people will do their duty without being ordered. But if he is not upright in his personal conduct, even though he gives orders, they will not be followed.

A man is ailing if he makes no progress in virtue, learns nothing new, abandons no bad habits and corrects no mistakes.

If a man improves himself, is he not indirectly improving his family, his country and ultimately the world?

Do not be in too much of a hurry to get things done; do not see only petty gains. If a man hurries too much, things will not be done thoroughly and well; if he sees only minor advantages, nothing great is accomplished.

A gentleman has a sense of shame, a sense of courtesy and a sense of right and wrong in the manner he conducts himself.

What do you say of a person who is loved by all the good people in his neighbourhood and is hated by all the bad people in his neighbourhood?

A virtuous man is easy to serve but difficult to please, for if you try to please him in any manner inconsistent with righteousness, he refuses to be pleased.

A gentleman has a dignified ease without pride; the mean person has pride without dignity or ease.

One who cherishes comfort and ease is not fit to be called a scholar.

In a country where good government prevails, a man should speak boldly and act boldly. But when a country is badly governed, though he acts boldly, let his speech be reserved.

A man of principle will always have something to say that is worth listening to, but men of words are not necessarily men of principle. He who cares for his fellowmen needs to be bold, but the bold may not necessarily care for their fellowmen.

It is possible to be a gentleman possessing great wealth and yet fail in philanthropy, but there is no such thing as a mean man who has philanthropy in him.

A gentleman may be loyal to others, but he does not refrain from admonishing the objects of his loyalty. Can he resist requiring much of those he loves?

The mind of a gentleman progresses upwards; the vulgar mind progresses downwards.

A man must do something worthy of mention when he has reached manhood. Merely to live on, getting older and older year by year, without having accomplished anything or getting any wiser, is to be a good-for-nothing.

In ancient times men studied for the sake of self-improvement; today they study to impress others.

A gentleman is ashamed to let his words outrun his deeds.

A man of superior mind can endure temptation unshaken; it is only the inferior person who becomes demoralised when submitted to temptation.

A great man does not grieve that others do not know him; he grieves at his own lack of ability.

A gentleman is considered so, not because of his height, but because of his character.

Is not he a gentleman who repays injury with kindness, and kindness with kindness?

To fail to speak to someone who is capable of learning is to lose an opportunity. To speak to someone who is incapable of benefitting is to waste your words. Those who are wise will not waste opportunities or words.

A gentleman demands much of himself; a mean man demands much of others.

He who takes no thought to problems in the future will be beset by worries before long.

A gentleman demands much of himself; a mean man demands much of others.

It is to be regretted if a party of people are together for a whole day without their conversation touching on what is right and wrong and if they take pleasure merely in shallow talk.

Is there one word which can be a guide to conduct throughout life? Is not Reciprocity such a word? What you do not want done to yourself, do not do to others.

In his judgement of others, a wise man does not easily assess blame, nor does he easily bestow praise.

When a leader is unpopular, it is necessary to inquire why people dislike him. When he is popular, it is also necessary to inquire why people like him.

A gentleman does not use clever talk to try and confound others.

In vain have I spent in thought a whole day without food and a whole night without sleep. I

*have found no advantage in this. I would have
done better to spend the time in learning.*

*A great man is capable of making Truth great; it
isn't Truth that makes a man great.*

*To a wise man, to err and not reform is indeed
abysmal folly.*

*One should devote one's mind to living a good and
full life, not merely living.*

*There are those who attain wisdom through
understanding, but if they lack benevolence, their
wisdom is of no avail. Again, there are those who
are wise and benevolent, but if they lack dignity,
they will not be revered. Lastly, there are those
who are wise, benevolent and dignified, but if they
do not act in accordance with the Rites, they are
still lacking in excellence.*

*A gentleman is devoted to principles; he is not
merely truthful.*

*A great man may not gain distinction in minor
matters, but he should be entrusted with important*

affairs. A man of average ability may gain distinction in minor matters, but he should not be entrusted with important affairs.

In the service of his country, a gentleman places duty first and reward last.

There is no point in men making plans together or taking counsel together who follow different ways.

In language, perspicuity is everything.

There are three kinds of friendship which do good and three which do harm. Friendship with upright men, with trustworthy men and with the well-learned, such friendships are beneficial. Friendship with men who are subtly perverse, with men who are artfully pliant and with glib-tongued men, such friendships are harmful.

There are three kinds of pleasure which do good and three which do harm. Pleasure derived from the regulation of the various branches of Ceremony and Music, pleasure in the appreciation and praise of virtue and pleasure in the company of wise men — these pleasures are beneficial. Pleasure from profligate enjoyment, from idle wandering and wild feasting — these are harmful.

There are three kinds of error to which a man is liable when in the presence of his superiors: first, to speak out when he is not called upon to speak — that is rashness; secondly, to keep silent when called upon to speak — that is foolish reticence; thirdly, to speak out without taking into consideration the expression on the face of the person spoken to — that is blindness.

There are three things a man should beware of: in youth, when his body is not yet fully developed and his strength not yet at its prime, he should guard against the urge of sex; in manhood, when his physical powers are matured, he should guard against an aggressive spirit; in old age, when his physical powers are declining, he should guard against any form of avarice and over-indulgence.

There are three things which a wise man holds in awe: he is in awe of the Decree of Heaven, the great on earth and the precepts of the sages. The

*mean man knows not the ordinances of Heaven
and therefore reveres them not, he treats the great
with contempt and he mocks the precepts of the
sages.*

*Those who are born wise are the highest type;
those who acquire wisdom through study rank next;
those who strive after it by hard study are third;
those who, although they study hard, never become
wise are the lowest.*

*There are nine things of which a man should be
mindful: to see clearly when he uses his eyes, to
hear distinctly when he uses his ears, to be
gracious in expression, to be respectful in
demeanour, to be sincere in speech, to be serious
in the execution of his duties, to seek advice when
in doubt, to consider the consequences when he is
angry, and to think of what is right and just when
he is faced with advantage or gain.*

*Those who, when they see what is good, try to live
up to it and hold fast to it, and when they see
what is evil, try to avoid it like scalding water —
such men I have heard of and known. But those*

who live in seclusion in order to attain goodness and practise right living — such men I have heard of, but never seen.

A wise father maintains a certain reserve towards his son.

Can a man be said to have benevolence towards his fellowmen who hoards the treasures of his knowledge and leaves his country the poorer?

By nature men are pretty much alike; it is their learning and practices that distinguish them.

There are six virtues and their attendant faults. First, there is kindness, but that alone without love of learning degenerates into fatuity. Secondly, there is knowledge, but that alone without love of learning tends to dilettantism. Thirdly, there is honesty, but that alone without love of learning produces heartlessness. Fourthly, there is uprightness, but that alone without love of learning leads to tyranny. Fifthly, there is boldness, but that alone without love of learning produces recklessness. Sixthly, there is strength of character, but that alone without love of learning produces wildness.

A gentleman is chary of venturing into the domain of those whose sharp tongues can upset kingdoms.

Be wary of permitting foreign music and dance to pervade and pervert the mind.

When one is in mourning, there is no relish in good food, no pleasure in music, no ease in the comforts of home.

It is bad to eat one's fill all day long but do nothing to feed the mind.

Moral education is of paramount importance. Righteousness should always come first. Bravery without righteousness could lead to crime.

A gentleman abhors those who talk about other people's misdeeds; who, occupying inferior positions, slander their superiors; who, possessing courage, lack the spirit of the Rites; who, though venturesome, are selfish and blind to reason; who are impulsive and yet believe themselves to be wise; who mistake insolence

for boldness; who cloak evil speaking with honesty.

If, after the age of forty, a man is still liked and respected by others, he will remain liked and respected all the days of his life.

One cannot herd birds with beasts. A man of worth mixes with worthy people.

A gentleman advances in learning with all earnestness, wishing to grasp the meaning of Truth within himself.

A gentleman does not treat those who are closely related to him in a casual manner, nor does he ignore their advice. Unless they have committed very serious faults, he does not abandon them. He does not expect anyone to be perfect.

He who from day to day knows exactly what he has yet to learn, and from month to month never forgets what he has learnt or mastered, is undoubtedly a true lover of learning.

Through wide learning and singleness of purpose, through keen questioning and searching of the heart, one may some day achieve greatness or even glory.

To master their trade, apprentices must labour in workshops; to acquire knowledge, a scholar must associate with men of learning and virtue. He should have only one regret, and that is when he neglects his studies.

When a gentleman makes a mistake, he never tries to gloss over it or whitewash his wrong-doing.

The gentleman creates three impressions: when seen from a distance, he is imposing in appearance; when approached, he is gracious; when heard speaking, his words are incisive.

A gentleman lays no burden on others until they have learned to trust him. Unless they trust him, they will feel that they are being exploited.

A true teacher does not confuse or mislead his students. He understands the beginning and end of learning and having commenced something, will see it through to the end.

When mourning for the death of his parents, a good son gives full expression to his grief.

The moral and intellectual endowments of ordinary men are like hills and mounds which are easily surmounted. But the moral and intellectual endowments of a gentleman are like the sun and moon over which no man can climb.

The faults of a great man may be compared to the eclipses of the sun and moon which are seen by all. But when he reforms, all men gaze at him with respect.

A man is judged wise by a single word he utters; equally, he is judged foolish by a single word he utters. That is why he must be cautions in what he says, so that while he lives he may be honoured by all men and when he dies he may be mourned by all men.

In order to inspire awe without being severe, a leader has to watch over every minute detail connected with his daily life, not only of conduct and bearing, but even of appearance and dress so as to produce a sense of respect in the public mind, which, though tantamount to fear, is in no way caused by it.

A good leader is not concerned about lack of wealth, but the equitable distribution of whatever wealth there may be. He is not concerned about poverty, but the insecurity of the poor. When there is fair distribution, there will be no poverty; when there is contentment, there will be no rebellion or revolution.

One phrase can sum up all the teachings of a gentleman: have no evil thoughts.

To lead in a righteous cause those who have not been instructed in the cause is to betray and destroy them.

A gentleman sets strict standards for himself, but makes allowances for others.

The benevolent man loves others, and the courteous man respects others. He who loves others is loved in return, and he who respects others is shown respect in return.

.... according to Mencius

*Benevolence, goodwill and righteousness should be
my only concern. What is the point of mentioning
the word 'profit'?*

*It is by sharing his wealth with the common people
that a leader is able to reign with success. Because
they share in his possessions, the people are willing
to die for him.*

*The attitude of a gentleman towards animals is
this: having once seen them alive, he cannot bear
to see them die; having once heard their cries, he
cannot bear to eat their flesh.*

*What virtue must one possess in order to become
a leader of men? If one loves and protects the
common people, there is no power except God
which can prevent one from attaining leadership.*

*Our land rightly belongs to those who came before
and those who will come after us. It is not ours to
dispose of freely. Let us defend it even unto death.*

The virtue of a just and benevolent man spreads

*faster than an order transmitted from posting
station to posting station.*

*There is neither good nor bad fortune which a
man does not bring upon himself. When God sends
down calamities, it is possible to escape them; but
when a man brings them upon himself, there is no
hope of escape.*

*A gentleman has a sensitive heart which cannot
bear to see suffering in others.*

*The feeling of compassion is the beginning of
benevolence; the feeling of shame and self-reproach,
the beginning of righteousness; the feeling of
courtesy and modesty, the beginning of propriety;
the feeling of right and wrong, the beginning of
wisdom. These four beginnings are like the four
limbs of man and to deny oneself any of these
potentialities is to cripple oneself.*

*A gentleman is like an archer who makes sure his
stance is correct before shooting an arrow. If he
fails to hit the mark, he does not hold it against
his victor, but seeks the cause of failure in himself.*

To accept from others that by which one can do good is to assist others to do good. There is nothing more important than helping others to do good.

Within a family, the most important relationship is between father and son. Within a country, the most important relationship is between the ruler and his subjects. In both relationships, the guiding principle is mutual love and respect.

To accept a gift without justification is tantamount to being bought. No gentleman should ever permit himself to be bought.

A good son will not for all the world be niggardly towards his parents.

The five great human relationships are between ruler and minister, between father and son, between husband and wife, between brothers and between friends.

To share one's wealth with others is generosity; to share with others when one is poor is an even greater virtue. To teach others to do good is conscientiousness; to do good oneself is an even greater virtue.

*Though a gentleman's mind is set on high ideals,
he never forgets that he may fall into a ditch;
though he is a man of valour, he never forgets that
he may lose his head.*

*A man has to live with himself; so he should see to
it that he is always good company.*

*Though he enjoys wealth and power, he is no
gentleman who has never studied the Rites. He may
live in splendid mansions, occupy high positions
and travel the highways of the world, but he
remains no gentleman.*

*A virtuous man cannot be led into excesses when
wealthy and honoured, or be deflected from his
purpose when poor and obscure. Nor can he be
made to bow before threats of violence.*

*A gentleman is indeed keen to
hold an office of high rank, but
he does not seek it by
dishonourable means.*

Do not wait until next year to

put an end to anything that is wrong or unrighteous now.

The compass and the carpenter's square are the ultimate measurement of the circle and the square. Wisdom is the ultimate measurement of human achievement.

If others do not respond to your love with love, look into your own heart; if others fail to respond to your attempts to teach and lead them, look into your own wisdom; if others do not return your courtesy, look into your own motives. In all cases, examine yourself whenever you fail to achieve your purpose.

Only when a family is disunited will others destroy it. Only when a country is disunited will others invade it.

If a man in a subordinate position fails to win the confidence of his superiors, he cannot hope to win promotion. He must find the way to win the confidence of his superiors. If his friends do not trust him, he will not win the confidence of his superiors. He must find the way to win the trust of his friends. If in serving his parents, he does not please them, he will not win the trust of his friends. He must find the way to please his parents. If upon looking within himself, he finds insincerity, he will not please his parents. He must learn to be sincere. If he cannot comprehend goodness, he cannot be sincere. Hence, the appreciation of goodness is the start of the Way.

There is in man nothing more ingenuous than the pupils of his eyes. He cannot conceal his wickedness. When he is upright, his eyes are clear and bright; when he is not, they are clouded and dull. How can a man conceal his true character if you listen well to his words and mark well the pupils of his eyes?

A leader possessing great wealth may be very liberal, but he may not know the art of ruling.

A man has to overcome all pettiness before he can achieve greatness. He must decide what he should not do, and then he is able to concentrate on what he should do.

A great man forever retains the heart of a child.

It is not enough to look after one's parents when they are living; it is important to honour and respect them even after they are dead.

One can never win the allegiance of others by trying to dominate them. One can only succeed by caring for their welfare.

The benevolent man loves others and the courteous man respects others. One who loves others is always loved by them; one who respects others is always respected by them.

Even when unexpected vexations come his way, a gentleman refuses to be perturbed by them.

Lack of filial piety has five causes: physical laziness, indulgence in frivolous pastimes like gambling and drinking, indulgence in sensual pleasures to the shame of one's parents, miserliness and selfishness, a quarrelsome and truculent nature. No gentleman should by guilty of these.

A wise man teaches his wife to respect his mother, and his mother to respect his wife.

A filial son yearns for his dead parents all his life. In this present generation, there are few who feel this way by the age of fifty.

In making friends with others, do not rely on the advantage of your age, rank or powerful connections. Friends are chosen for their virtue, nothing else.

An inferior person showing deference to a superior person is honouring the honoured. A superior person showing deference to an inferior person is honouring the good and wise. Both are equally important.

A gentleman communes not only with his contemporaries but also with the best gentlemen of antiquity. As he reads their poems and writings, he comes to understand them and the age in which they lived. In this way he aspires to friends in past ages.

Human nature resembles running water. Open an outlet to the east and it will flow east, let it out on

*the west and it will flow west. So human nature
does not show any preference for good or evil, just
as water is indifferent to east or west. The fact that
man can be influenced for good or evil shows that
his nature is no different from water in this respect.*

*When his chickens and dogs stray, a man has
sense enough to go after them. Should he therefore
not be even more diligent in pursuit if his heart
strays from the path of truth and goodness?*

*All that can be expected of all men is benevolence.
Though they follow different paths, their goal
should be the same, and that is simply benevolence.*

*A man is entitled to hold office not by virtue of his
birth but of his worth, and different offices should
not be held concurrently by the same person.*

*There is goodness out of adversity. Exhaustion,
hunger, hardship, poverty, bitterness and frustration
will stimulate a man's mind, toughen his character
and make good his defects.*

*To act without clear understanding, to form habits
without examining them, to pursue the Way all his*

life without knowing where it leads — such is the way of the ignorant man.

A gentleman must not be without shame, for the shame of being without shame is indeed shamelessness.

Benevolent words do not have as profound an effect as benevolent deeds. Good government does not win the common people so much as does moral education. Good government secures the wealth of the people; moral education secures their hearts.

Rectify the mistakes in others by first rectifying them in yourself.

A gentleman has three delights: that his parents are alive and well and his family free from anxiety; that he need feel no shame before God and no embarrassment before his fellowmen; that it is his to teach and train the most talented pupils in the land.

One with definite aims to accomplish may be compared to a man digging a well. To dig to a depth of seventy-two cubits and stop without reaching the spring is, after all, to throw away the well.

To feed a man without showing him love is to treat him like a pig; to love him without showing him respect is to keep him like a domestic animal. Love and respect are gifts for the giving. But without sincerity, they are an empty show.

A bad year cannot starve one who has accumulated sufficient wealth; a wicked generation cannot confound one who has laid up a full store of virtue.

Enlighten others by being learned and wise. You cannot help others if you remain in benighted ignorance.

One who commands our liking is what is called a good man. One whose goodness is part of himself is called a truthful man. One who is filled with goodness is called a virtuous man. One whose complete goodness can be seen by all is called a great man. When this great man exercises a transforming influence, he is what is called a sage. When the sage is virtuous beyond our comprehension, he becomes a spiritual man.

A good leader prizes three treasures highly: the country, the people and orderly government. Calamity faces the leader who treasures pearls and jade instead.

To have a good knowledge of men is the proper qualification of a gentleman; to have a sound knowledge of political affairs is the proper qualification of a leader.

To shame one's personal name is bad enough, but to shame one's surname is unforgivable because a surname is shared with others.

Treat the aged in your family with the considera-tion and respect they deserve and extend this treat-ment to the aged of other people's families. Treat the young in your family with the kindness they

deserve and extend this treatment to the young people in other peo-ple's families.

When our senses are exercised without thought and are thereby obscured by material things, we are led astray. Heaven gave us mind and senses. Guided by thought, let us use our senses in the right way.

If a man build up the nobler part of his nature, then the baser part cannot overcome it.

All things are already complete in man. There is no greater delight than to find, on self-examination, that one is true to oneself.

Altruism is the shortest and surest road to humanity. Humanity is the distinguishing characteristic of mankind.

.... according to Others

A gentleman is a man who can disagree without being disagreeable.

Anonymous

He would be the finer gentleman that leaves the world untainted with falsehood, or dissimulation, or wantonness, or conceit.

Marcus Aurelius

He is a Gentleman, because his nature Is kind and affable to every creature.

Richard Barnfield

Meet success like gentleman and disaster like a man.

Lord Birkenhead

A gentleman is one who thinks more of other people's feelings than his own rights; and more of other people's rights than his own feelings.

Matthew Henry Buckham

Somebody has said that a king may make a nobleman, but he cannot make a gentleman.

Edmund Burke

The gentleman is a Christian product.

George G. Calvert

A gentleman has ease without familiarity, is respectful without meanness, genteel without affectation.

Lord Chesterfield

The true pleasures of a gentleman are those of the table, but within the bound of moderation; good company, that is to say, people of merit; moderate play which amuses, without any interested views; and sprightly gallant conversations with women of fashion and sense.

Lord Chesterfield

If a man's mind is erroneously possessed with the idea that he is a great violinist, that need not prevent his being a gentleman and an honest man. But if once his mind is possessed in any strong degree with the knowledge that he is a gentleman, he will soon cease to be one.

G.K. Chesterton

49

There is no such thing as being a gentleman at important moments; it is at unimportant moments that a man is a gentleman. At important moments he ought to be something better.

G.K. Chesterton

You may depend upon it, religion is, in its essence, the most gentlemanly thing in the world. It will, alone, gentilize, if unmixed with cant; and I know nothing else which, alone, will.

Samuel Taylor Coleridge

Little ladies may be born, but little gentlemen are hewn, like monuments, out of solid resistance.

Marcelene Cox

A man can never be a true gentleman in manner until he is a true gentleman at heart.

Charles Dickens

Propriety of manners and consideration for others are the two main characteristics of a gentleman.

Disraeli

A gentleman must be incapable of a lie.

Ralph Waldo Emerson

A gentleman makes no noise; a lady is serene.
                                    Ralph Waldo Emerson

*The flowering of civilization is the finished man,
the man of sense, of grace, of accomplishment, of
social power — the gentleman.*
                                    Ralph Waldo Emerson

*Education begins a gentleman; conversation
completes him.*
                                            Thomas Fuller

*One of the marks of a gentleman is his refusal to
make an issue out of every difference of opinion.*
                                    Arnold H. Glasgow

*A gentleman is one who understands and shows
every mark of deference to the claims of self-love
in others, and exacts it in return from them.*
                                            William Hazlitt

*Hence it is almost a definition of a gentleman to
say that he is one .... (see attached sheet)*
                                    John Henry, Cardinal Newman

The quality of a gentleman is so very fine a thing that it seems to me one should not be at all hasty in concluding that one possesses it.

Gerald Manley Hopkins

Thoughtfulness for others, generosity, modesty and self-respect are the qualities which make a real gentleman or lady, as distinguished from the veneered article which commonly goes by that name.

Thomas Henry Huxley

A man may learn from his Bible to be a more thorough gentleman than if he had been brought up in all the drawing-rooms in London.

Charles Kingsley

A gentleman is a gardener who can call a spade a spade without adding any qualifying adjectives.

Albert D. Lasseter

The gentleman does not needlessly and unnecessarily remind an offender of a wrong he may have committed against him. He not only can forgive, he can forget; and he strives for that nobleness of self

*and mildness of character which impart sufficient
strength to let the past be but the past. A true man
of honour feels humbled himself when he cannot
help humbling others.*

Robert E. Lee

*Education begins the gentleman, but reading, good
company and reflection must finish him.*

John Locke

*Hence it is almost a definition of a gentleman to
say he is one who never inflicts pain. The true
gentleman in like manner carefully avoids whatever
may jar or jolt the minds of those with whom he
is cast — all clashing of opinion, or collision of
feeling, all restraint, or suspicion, or gloom, or
resentment — his great concern being to make
every one at ease and at home. He has his eyes on
all his company; he is tender towards the bashful,
gentle towards the distant, and merciful towards the
absurd; he can recollect to whom he is speaking; he
guards against unreasonable allusions, or topics
which may irritate; he is seldom prominent in
conversation, and never wearisome. He makes light
of favours while he does them, and seems to be*

*receiving when he is conferring. He never speaks of
himself except when compelled, never defends
himself by a mere retort, he has no ears for slander
or gossip, is scrupulous in imputing motives to
those who interfere with him, and interprets
everything for the best. He is never mean or little in
his disputes, never takes unfair advantage, never
mistakes personalities or sharp sayings for
arguments, or insinuates evil which he dare not say
out. From a long-sighted prudence, he observes the
maxim of the ancient sage, that we should ever
conduct ourselves towards our enemy as if he were
one day to be our friend. He has too much good
sense to be affronted at insults, he is too well
employed to remember injuries, and too indolent to
bear malice. He is patient, forbearing, and resigned
on philosophical principles; he submits to pain,
because it is inevitable to bereavement, because it is
irreparable, and to death, because it is his destiny.
If he engages in controversy of any kind, his
disciplined intellect preserves him from the blunder-
ing discourtesy of better though less educated minds
who, like blunt weapons, tear and hack instead of
cutting clean, who mistake the point in argument,
waste their strength on trifles, misconceive their
adversary, and leave the question more involved*

*than they find it. He may be right or wrong in his
opinion, but he is too clear-headed to be unjust; he
is as simple as he is forcible, and as brief as he is
decisive. Nowhere shall we find greater candour,
consideration, indulgence; he throws himself into the
minds of his opponents, he accounts for their
mistakes. He knows the weakness of human reason
as well as its strength, its province and its limits. If
he be an unbeliever, he will be too profound and
large-minded to ridicule religion or to act against it;
he is too wise to be a dogmatist or fanatic in his
infidelity. He respects piety and devotion; he even
supports institutions as venerable, beautiful, or
useful, to which he does not assent; he honours the
ministers of religion, and he is contented to decline
its mysteries without assailing or denouncing them.
He is a friend of religious toleration, and that, not
only because his philosophy has taught him to look
on all forms of faith with an impartial eye, but also
from the gentleness and effeminacy of feeling,
which is the attendant on civilisation.*

John Henry, Cardinal Newman

*The gentleman is a man of culture, a man of
refinement, above all an honest man possessing that
good taste which is the conscience of the mind, that*

conscience which is the good taste of the soul.
                                        James Russell Lowell

A gentleman is one who never strikes a woman, without provocation.

                                        H.L. Mencken

This is the final test of a gentleman: his respect for those who can be of no possible service to him.
                                        William Lyon Phelps

Anyone can be heroic from time to time, but a gentleman is something you have to be all the time — which isn't easy.

                                        Luigi Pirandello

Far more important than any mere dictum of etiquette is the fundamental code of honour, without strict observance of which no man, no matter how 'polished', can be considered a gentleman. The honour of a gentleman demands the inviolability of his word, and the incorruptibility of his principles. He is the descendant of the knight, the crusader; he is the defender of the defenceless and the champion of justice — or he is not a gentleman.

                                        Emily Post

A gentleman's first characteristic is that fineness of structure in the body which renders it capable of the most delicate sensations; and of structure in the mind which renders is capable of the most delicate sympathies — one may say, simply, 'fineness of nature'.

John Ruskin

Gentleman, in its primal, literal and perpetual meaning, is a man of pure race.

John Ruskin

Gentlemanliness, being another word for intense humanity.

John Ruskin

Gentlemen have to learn that it is no part of their duty or privilege to live on other people's toil; that there is no degradation in the hardest manual or the humblest servile labour, when it is honest.

John Ruskin

One never thinks of Habukkuk, John the Baptist, Epictetus, Martin Luther or Calvin as gentlemen; they were prophets, saints, heroes, if you like, but not gentlemen.

H.D. Sedgwick

I am a gentleman of blood and breeding.
                    William Shakespeare, 'King Lear'

We are gentlemen,
That neither in our hearts, nor outward eyes
Envy the great, nor do the low despise.
                    William Shakespeare, 'Pericles'

A gentleman of our days is one who has money
enough to do what every fool would do if he could
afford it; that is, consume without producing.
                    George Bernard Shaw

It is a grand old name, that of gentleman, and has
been recognized as a rank and power in all stages
of society. To possess this character is a dignity of
itself, commanding the instinctive homage of every
generous mind, and those who will not bow to
titular rank will yet do homage to the gentleman.
His qualities depend not upon fashion or manners,
but upon moral worth; not on personal possessions,
but on personal qualities.
                    Samuel Smiles

He has achieved success who has lived well,
laughed often and loved much; who has gained the

*respect of intelligent men and the love of little
children; who has filled his niche and accomplished
his task; who has left the world better than he
found it, whether by an improved poppy, a perfect
poem, or a redeemed soul; who has never lacked
appreciation of earth's beauty, or failed to express
it; who has always looked for the best in others
and given the best he had; whose life was an
inspiration; whose memory is a benediction.*

Bessie A. Stanley

*Men of courage, men of sense and men of letters
are frequent; but a true gentleman is what one
seldom sees.*

Sir Richard Steele

*Perhaps a gentleman is a rarer man than some of
us think; for which of us can point out many such
in his circle — men whose aims are generous,
whose truth is not only constant in its kind but
elevated in its degree; whose want of meanness
makes them simple; who can look the world honest-
ly in the face with an equal manly sympathy for
the great and the small.*

William Makepeace Thackeray

To be a gentleman is to be honest, to be gentle, to be generous, to be brave, to be wise and possessing all those qualities, to exercise them in the most graceful outward manner.

William Makepeace Thackeray

Who misses or wins the prize,
Go lose or conquer as you can;
But if you fail or if you rise,
Be each, pray God, a gentleman.

William Makepeace Thackeray

My experience has been that the time to test a true gentleman is to observe him when he is in contact with individuals of a race that is less fortunate than his own.

Booker T. Washington

If a man is a gentleman, he knows quite enough, and if he is not a gentleman, whatever he knows is bad for him.

Oscar Wilde

A gentleman? ... Individual conscience will rule his social acts. By love of quality as against quantity he will choose his way through life. He will learn